HOW TO SOOTHE YOUR MINGE RASH WITHOUT SETTING YOUR PANTS ON FIRE

A HILARIOUS GAG GIFT FOR ANYONE WHO NEEDS A LAUGH

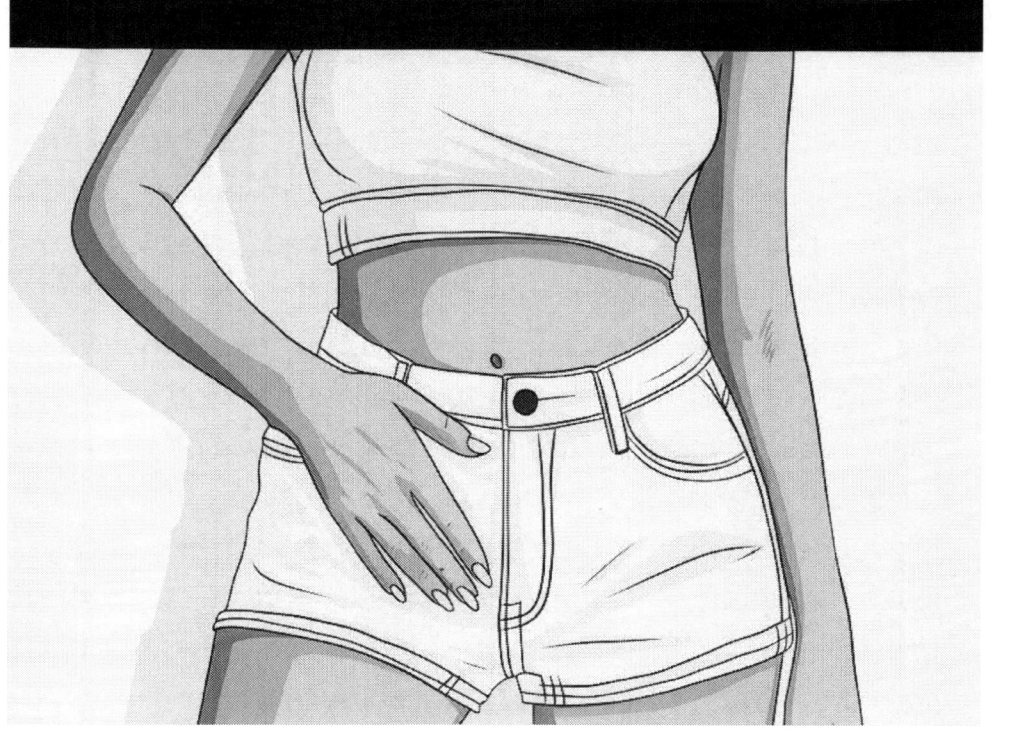

Copyright © 2024 . All rights reserved.

Legal Notice

The content of this book is protected by copyright law. It is intended for personal use only. No part of this book may be reproduced, duplicated, transmitted, modified, distributed, sold, used, quoted, or paraphrased without the express written permission of the author or publisher. Any unauthorized use is strictly prohibited. The author and publisher accept no responsibility for any damages, reparations, or monetary losses arising from the use of the information contained in this book, whether directly or indirectly.

Disclaimer

The information provided in this book is for educational and entertainment purposes only. Every effort has been made to ensure the accuracy, reliability, and completeness of the information presented. However, no warranties, either express or implied, are made regarding the content. The author is not providing legal, financial, medical, or professional advice. Readers should consult with a licensed professional before attempting any techniques described in this book. By reading this book, the reader agrees that the author will not be liable for any losses or damages, direct or indirect, resulting from the use of the information contained herein, including but not limited to errors, omissions, or inaccuracies.

Introduction

Because Life's Too Short to Take Your Rash (or Yourself) Too Seriously

Welcome, intrepid reader, to the book you didn't know you needed—or perhaps you really did. Whether this was a self-purchase or a gift from a "friend" who probably deserves a punch in the arm, you're holding a treasure trove of absurdity. This book isn't here to heal you; it's here to make you laugh while you awkwardly scratch in public.

Let's be clear: this isn't a serious guide. If you've been frantically Googling remedies for your minge mishap, it's time to put down your phone and pick up some ointment (or see an actual doctor, please). This book is for everyone who's ever faced life's little irritations—be they literal, like your rash, or metaphorical, like that coworker who chews loudly in meetings.

Inside, you'll find 55 ridiculous, totally impractical, and delightfully over-the-top ways to soothe your minge rash without setting your pants—or your dignity—on fire. No guarantees, no refunds, and absolutely no promises of medical accuracy.

So, scratch (or don't) your way to the first page and get ready to laugh. Because if you can't laugh at life's awkward moments, what can you do? Probably itch.

Enjoy the chaos,
Itchingly Yours,
The Totally Unqualified Authors of This Masterpiece

Medical Disclaimer

Because We're Not Doctors (and Neither Is This Book)

This book is absolutely not a substitute for professional medical advice. If you're dealing with an actual rash, we highly recommend consulting a doctor, dermatologist, or even that overly helpful pharmacist who loves to give unsolicited advice—not this collection of sarcastic nonsense masquerading as "helpful tips."

The ideas in these pages are for entertainment purposes only. We repeat: ENTERTAINMENT ONLY. If you try any of these so-called "remedies" and end up itchier, redder, or somehow questioning your entire existence, that's 100% on you. Honestly, what did you expect?

In short: If things go from bad to worse (or itchier), don't point the finger at us. Instead, thank the "friend" who thought this book was the perfect gift for you.

Now, laugh responsibly, apply some cream (the real kind), and maybe rethink your social circle.

"Ice It Out"

When you feel the burn, grab a popsicle, because nothing says "relief" like cooling your nether regions and pretending you're on vacation.

"The Hairdryer Method"

Blasting your sensitive bits with hot air might not be a genius move, but it'll certainly make you question your life choices.

"Use the Yoga Pose"

Assume the downward dog near an open window—air out the situation and pray for the best.

"Toothpaste Is Your Friend (Or Not)"

Slather that minty, cool paste and feel the burn... or just accept it as the price of fresh breath.

"DIY Mud Mask"

Rub mud on it like you're some kind of spa guru, because why not make it even worse?

"The Classic Ice Pack"

Apply it and try not to scream when it turns into a makeshift torture device.

"The Paper Towel Solution"

Wrap yourself in paper towels like a DIY mummy; it's either going to work or you'll just get confused looks.

"Cucumber Cool-Down"

Slap those cucumber slices on and convince yourself you're at a fancy spa, because reality's overrated.

"Essential Oils: Just Smell Good"

Rub on some lavender and pretend your rash is a wellness retreat. Spoiler: It's not.

"The Hair Conditioner Strategy"

Lather it up and say you're trying to make peace with your skin. Who said it's just for hair?

"Cooler Than You"

Place an ice cube in a strategic spot, because nothing says relief like a surprise cold snap.

"The Frozen Peas Trick"

Sit on them and pretend you're making a modern art piece; you're just here for the cool vibes.

"The Fan of Regret"

Set up a fan to blow air where you need it most and just accept that your hair will now be a wild mess.

"Get Holy with It"

Call the priest, because at this point, you need divine intervention.

"Aloe Vera Overload"

Apply so much that you're basically a walking aloe plant. It's hydrating... or is it?

"Peppermint Power"

Rub peppermint oil on it; if you're lucky, it'll feel tingly instead of like a firework show.

"The Fanning Frenzy"

Use a fan to provide that much-needed breeze. It's not therapy, but it'll do.

"Baking Soda Buff"

Dust yourself in baking soda and say you're making a cookie. Spoiler: You're not.

"Hot Tea for the Win"

Place a warm, damp tea bag down there and pretend you're sipping at a 19th-century tea party.

"The 'Don't Touch' Method"

Just don't. It's better this way. Pretend it's a no-touch zone.

"The Vodka Dab"

Dab some vodka down there—it'll sting, but at least you'll forget why you did it.

"The 'Never-Ending' Fan"

Sit in front of a fan on high speed; it's like a wind tunnel for your crotch. Get ready for that wild, "I'm too cool for this" look.

"Frozen Fruit Pack"

Why settle for peas when you can use a bag of frozen mango chunks? It's fruity, it's cool, and it's definitely weird.

. "The Sunburn Strategy"

Lay out in the sun, but only if you want to feel like you're turning into a lizard. At least you'll have a story.

"Hot Tea Compress"

Steep some tea, let it cool, and then hold the warm tea bag to the area. Feel the zen, or just the regret.

"Baking Soda Blitz"

Dust a layer of baking soda on and pray it doesn't look like an accidental snowstorm.

"The Chamomile Chill"

Saturate a cloth in chamomile tea and pat it on. It's so soothing you might even forget you're in pain.

"Spicy Sauce Scream"

Splash on some hot sauce for that extra zing. Just kidding, don't do that.

"Coconut Oil Comfort"

Slather on coconut oil and get ready to shine. You'll look like you're ready for a summer commercial.

"Lavender Levitations"

Drop some lavender oil on a hot compress, let it soak, and wonder why you didn't think of this sooner.

"Sprinkle That Magic Powder"

Dust yourself with baby powder as if you're the next big thing in a powder advertisement. It'll be dry and uncomfortable—just how you like it.

"Minty Relief"

Rub a generous amount of minty balm on it and experience the cool sensation that makes you question why you did this to yourself.

"Bubble Wrap Bash"

Wrap yourself in bubble wrap; at the very least, you'll be too busy popping it to feel the rash.

"Hot Sauce Adventure"

Dare to rub a tiny bit of hot sauce on it. Spoiler alert: It's more painful than a breakup.

"The Lotion Layering"

Slather on a thick layer of lotion and tell yourself it's for hydration. Spoiler: It's just greasy.

"The Ice Cream Relief"

Sit with a bowl of ice cream on your lap, and at least the suffering will feel like a pleasant distraction.

"Spritz and Pray"

Use a spritz of cooling body spray; it might do nothing, but at least you'll smell good while you're uncomfortable.

"Frozen Banana Hack"

Try sitting on a frozen banana; it'll feel awkward and cold, but hey, it's better than nothing.

"Fan Club Member"

Sit with a mini handheld fan blowing directly on it; you might look ridiculous, but at least you're cool.

NEVER FORGET The Power of Breeze.

"The Cold Cucumber"

Use a cucumber slice and pretend you're a salad in progress. Bonus points if you invite friends over.

"Sage Smudging Ritual"

Burn sage and chant some good vibes; it's either going to work or just give you a smoky house.

"Glitter Bomb"

Sprinkle glitter for a bit of sparkle in your life; it's a party and a rash solution all in one.

IT'S NOT EVEN NEW YEAR'S.

"The Peppermint Foot Rub"

Rub peppermint oil on your feet and hope the coolness travels upward. Spoiler: It won't, but your feet will be fresh.

"The Water Balloon Trick"

Fill a balloon with water and gently sit on it, feeling like you're in an oddly specific spa treatment.

"The Spa Day Fantasy"

Cover yourself in a mix of yogurt and honey for that "luxury treatment" you never asked for. Bonus: You'll smell like a snack.

"The 'Dry as a Bone' Strategy"

Use baby powder until you're so dry you could be mistaken for a desert. No moisture, no problem

"Lemon Zest Blast"

Rub some lemon zest on it. It'll sting, but at least you'll be revitalized, right?

"The Double Duty Deal"

Sit on a bag of frozen peas and watch your face go from pain to confusion as it thaws.

"The Aloe Vera Slather"

Go full-on aloe and hope for the best. It's soothing, until it turns into a sticky, green mess.

"Coconut Oil Overkill"

Drown in coconut oil and pray you don't slide out of your chair. Smells great, but it's like a slip-and-slide.

CAUTION: SLIPPERY WHEN WET!

"The DIY Ice Bath"

Fill a tub with ice and water, and make the most questionable decision of your life. It'll shock your system and remind you that life is pain.

"The Spice Is Right"

Try rubbing chili powder on it for that "spicy" thrill. Just kidding, don't. Your future self will hate you.

"The Frozen Grape Party"

Take some frozen grapes, let them thaw for a few minutes, and pray that they feel good on contact.

"Cold Compress Command"

Wrap your sensitive area in a cold compress and try not to imagine you're in an icy dungeon.

"The Charcoal Remedy"

Charcoal for detoxing? Slather it on and wonder if you're now an exclusive club member of the "I regret everything" group.

"The Humidifier Heaven"

Turn up your humidifier to max, sit under it, and pray the mist makes you forget your discomfort.

Printed in Great Britain
by Amazon